instant gratification
jewelry

instant gratification jewelry

FAST & FABULOUS PROJECTS

by Annie Guthrie | Photography by Julie Toy

CHRONICLE BOOKS

SAN FRANCISCO

Library of Congress Cataloging-in-Publication Data:
Guthrie, Annie.
Jewelry : fast & fabulous projects / by Annie Guthrie ; photography by Julie Toy
p. cm— (Instant gratification)

ISBN 0-8118-2686-4
1.   Jewelry making. I. Title. II. Series
TT212.G88 2000
745.594′2—dc21
00-022422

Printed in Hong Kong.

Prop styling by Gia Russo
Designed by Level
Typesetting by Level
The photographer wishes to thank Aimee Adams and Philip Morrison.

Distributed in Canada by Raincoast Books
9050 Shaughnessy Street
Vancouver, British Columbia V6P 6E5

1 3 5 7 9 10 8 6 4 2

Chronicle Books LLC
85 Second Street
San Francisco, California 94105

www.chroniclebooks.com

THE FIRST BOOK IS FOR MY DARLING MOTHER,

and all my other loved ones—you know who you are.

table of

contents

introduction

Welcome to the knob on the door to the world of beading. As centuries of beading tradition stretch into millennia, this "world" is becoming more like a universe, one in which the beginner can quickly get lost. This book attempts to throw you a line, and guide you through astronomically varying choices in materials and designs. The goal is to lure you into feeling proud—quickly, in hopes that you might begin to want to spend more time in our orbit.

The *Instant Gratification* series assumes you are a busy working person who is feeling creative and searching for a new outlet. We hope we can take the edge off the task of learning something new. Each project is made up of a maximum of seven easy steps, and the necessary beads can be easily located at any bead store.

If you want to make a new necklace or a pair of earrings, you will find that the book is easily referenced: each section is organized by category. The first section, "The Goods," will tell you what you need to know about the basic materials you'll require. In addition, there are a few basic beading techniques that you will use again and again; you can find these highlighted in "Techniques—Up Close," page 14.

There are thirty-eight projects to choose from, but feel free to depart from these designs to substitute beads or incorporate different techniques in order to discover your own personal aesthetic. Good luck, and have fun in your designing endeavors!

the goods

FIRST LET'S TAKE A CLOSER LOOK AT SOME OF THE INDIVIDUAL COMPONENTS YOU WILL NEED TO BEGIN YOUR BEADING ADVENTURE.

BEADS While for me the charm and mystery of learning beadwork lies in the history of the beads themselves, this book is for the beginning designer, and so I have chosen to use relatively new, inexpensive beads that can be easily found or for which there are convenient substitutes. For example, Balinese, Indian, and Thai silver beads are relatively inexpensive and readily available. You will also find semi-precious glass beads abundant in any bead store. In some cases you'll see I call for a strand of beads; this is a standard measurement. At the back of the book I have listed suppliers close to my heart whose beads I used in this book. I encourage you to find a new home in your local bead store. Keep an eye out for trade shows in your area, where you can always get a good deal on beads and findings and talk directly with the dealers, many of whom have had contact with the families or artisans where the goods originated.

I do strongly encourage beginning beaders to find out all they can about the beads they are using; the jewelry is all the more desirable if the designer is familiar with and fond of its components. There are a few books I admire on the history and construction of the beads themselves, listed in "Resources" at the back of the book.

tools & materials

CHAIN (a) Sections of chain can be easily incorporated into any design to add texture and weight. In addition, chain can be used to extend the length of a necklace—make sure to choose a chain whose holes are large enough for the clasp to fit through. Chain is available in all metals: nickel, brass, copper, sterling, and gold. You may wish to oxidize the chain to achieve an antique finish.

FILES (not pictured) Tiny beading files are optional, but clean edges really add a dash of professionalism to your pieces. Use them to file burrs off the ends of your links or handmade clasps. *Always* use them on the push stroke—that is, file in one direction, away from you. (If you slide files back and forth across the metal, you will destroy them.)

GLUE (not pictured) Look for a glue that will bind fabric and glass as well as metals. For our purposes, I have used Hypo-Cement because the cap includes a needle with a fine point so you can drop the glue more precisely. You may also use clear nail polish to reinforce knotted thread.

HARD-NOSE PLIER (f) Use these to manipulate jump or split rings (see Findings, pages 12 and 13) or to bend heavy-gauge wire. Unlike round-nose pliers, they will not make teeth marks in the metal.

MANDREL OR DOWEL (not pictured) Mandrels come in different sizes; for wire work purposes, the smaller the diameter, the better. Use a mandrel or dowel to make clasps or jump rings (see Findings, page 12) or to help guide any curve in a bracelet or other type of jewelry.

MEMORY WIRE (d) Memory wire retains its shape and comes in standard neck, wrist, and ring sizes. Use this tough, resilient wire to make beaded chokers, bracelets, and rings.

NEEDLES (b) There are so many needles to choose from that the possibilities can be overwhelming for a beginning beader. As you progress along the beading path, you will need to know that sizes 10, 12, 13, 15, and 16 get smaller (thinner) as the number gets larger. Where possible, I have recommended using twisted wire needles—they are flexible, and their big eyes makes them easy to thread. You can get away with using a size 12 for the projects in this book, or you can use an embroidery needle to take larger-holed beads through felt, leather, or chamois. In most cases, it will be easiest to use the largest needle that will fit through your smallest-holed bead.

NIPPERS OR CUTTERS (g) Nippers with fine points are essential for

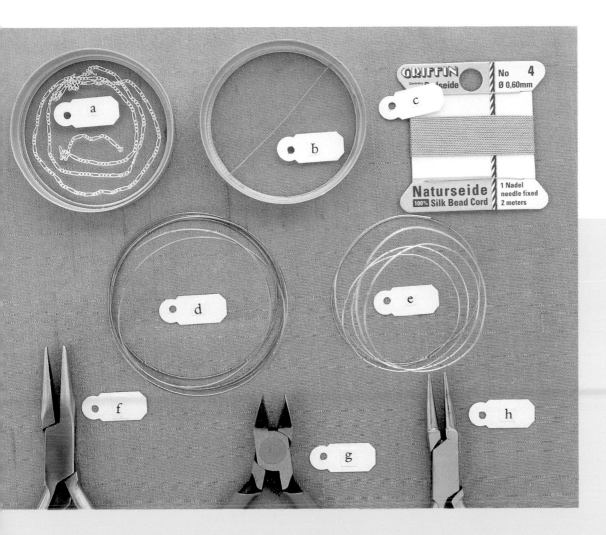

GRIFFIN
Germany
c
No 4
Ø 0,60mm

Naturseide
100% Silk Bead Cord
1 Nadel
needle fixed
2 meters

getting in close to those pesky wire tail ends. Flush cutters are less precise but cut a cleaner edge; they are useful for cutting heavy-gauge wire.

ROUND-NOSE PLIERS (h) You can find these in varying diameters. Use their smooth curves to guide wire into any loop, arc, or bow.

THREAD (c) There is a range of threads to choose from, including silk, nylon, and elastic. Beginning beaders favor thread cards (thread wrapped around small cards) but you might want to invest in larger spools as you progress. Nylon is stronger than silk, but silk comes in a wider selection of colors.

WIRE (e) Wire comes in varying sizes, shapes, degrees of flexibility, and colors. Where beadwork is concerned, you might use any size ranging from 16- to 26-gauge; the lower the number, the thicker the wire. You can choose from round, square, half-round, soft or half-hard, gold-fill, sterling, nickel, copper, steel, and brass.

BARRETTE BACKS (i) Use wire thread to wrap around these backings, or glue material of choice (such as felt, leather, or suede) over them.

BEAD CAPS (j) These can be decorative or functional. Bead caps dress up any plain glass bead or can hide knots of multiple stranded necklaces.

BEAD TIPS (k) Use these to finish jewelry that is strung on thread. Knots are hidden inside the cup, and the hook attaches to a jump ring or clasp.

CLASPS (l) There are many types of clasps you can use as closures for your jewelry—hooks-and-eyes, S-clasps, lobsters, spring rings. Choose according to size, style, metal, or level of safety.

CRIMP BEADS (m) Some materials won't knot without snapping; crimp beads are used to keep loops secure in coated wire or mono-filament. They come in varying shapes and metals.

findings

EARRING FINDINGS (n) Most earring findings—French hooks, kidney wires, ball-and-post—come with a loop through which you can attach any headpin or chain link. Choose your finding according to preferred length and style.

HEADPINS (o) Headpins are a beginning beader's dream come true. These wire pieces end in a nail head, so you can easily turn your favorite beads into a favorite pair of earrings. Make your own with 22- or heavier-gauge wire, or buy pre-made headpins with a nail-head or loop end. Use these to make pendants or earrings.

HOOPS (p) Hoop findings are made from a harder metal to help retain their shape. You can add beads or beaded headpins directly onto the unlooped end.

JUMP RINGS (q) These rings are most often used to attach the ends of chain or threaded pieces to a clasp. Some people incorporate them into their designs. Make your own jump rings on a mandrel or

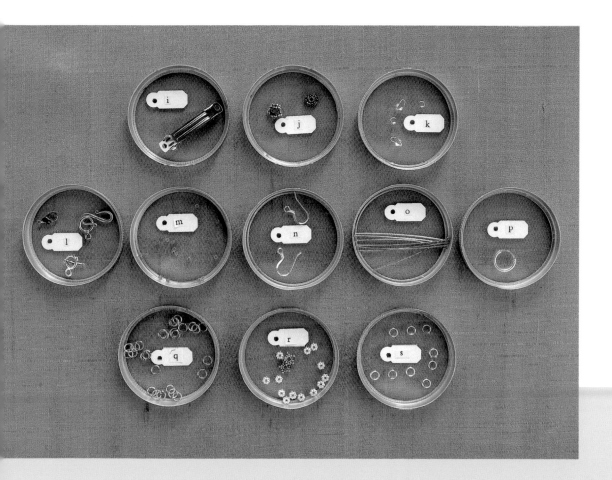

simply using round-nose pliers. Open them sideways, using hard-nose pliers, rather than pulling them apart. This will ensure that the ring keeps its strength and shape.

SPACER BEADS (r) Spacers are used to offset or emphasize any other bead. The beads most often referred to as spacers in this book are flat Balinese "daisies." Spacer bars have more than one hole and are used to keep multiple-stranded necklaces from twisting, or to help keep the strands in a graduated necklace separated.

SPLIT RINGS (s) Use these to attach clasps or heavy pendants. Split rings open like a key ring and provide a more secure closure than jump rings. The smaller they are, the more difficult they will be to open.

optional accessories

BEADING BOARD Laying out your design *before* you begin beading will save you lots of time. Beading boards are useful because they are marked off in inches, and they have separate compartments for multiple strands, allowing you to plan exactly where each bead will fall. A sheet of velvet or a towel is an acceptable substitute.

BEADING DISHES Some people get just as excited about containers for beads as they do about the beads themselves. Ideally, your dishes will be low-sided with a lip, and heavy enough that they won't tip over.

techniques—up close

HERE ARE A FEW BASIC BEADING TECHNIQUES YOU WILL NEED TO LEARN IN ORDER TO COMPLETE MOST OF THE PROJECTS.

ADDING A CLASP Add a clasp to nearly any necklace by adding a jump or split ring to the ends of the necklace. Open the ring sideways and slip it through the loop or link at the end of the necklace, then slip it through the loop in the clasp, and close the ring. See more under "Opening Jump Rings and Links," page 17.

CRIMPING Crimp beads are used to help clasp the ends of nylon wire such as Beadalon or Soft Flex. Add a crimp bead to one end of the wire. Take the end through an end ring or clasp and loop back through the crimp bead. Smash the bead with hard-nose pliers.

KNOTTING INSIDE A BEAD TIP To finish a necklace, add a bead tip after the last bead. Make a loose knot. Insert your tweezers *through* the knot and place them deep inside the bead tip. The farther down into the bead tip you pull the knot, the less slack in the necklace there will be. Pull taut. The knot will slip around the tip of the tweezers and settle at the point.

KNOTTING WITH TWEEZERS Make a loose knot. Place your tweezers *through* the knot and grab the thread in the place you want the knot to sit. Wherever you place the tweezers is where the knot will sit. You can also try this with round-nose pliers.

MAKING BEAD CHARMS It is easy to turn beads into charms using headpins and round-nose pliers. Slip a bead, or a combination of

beads, onto a headpin. The pinlike base of the headpin prevents the bead from sliding off the wire. Using round-nose pliers, grasp the wire just above the bead and curl the wire tail around the pliers, forming a loop. Wrap the wire around the pliers rather than trying to force it with the pliers. Straighten loop and tail so the loop is centered on the wire. Grab loop between hard-nose pliers and wind the tail around the headpin, just above the loop, with your fingers. Snip off excess wire so that there are an equal number of wraps on each side.

MAKING A WIRE LOOP Place round-nose pliers on the end of the wire and curl. Try to wrap the wire around the pliers rather than attacking it with the pliers; this will cut down on teeth marks made by the pliers. Straighten the loop using hard-nose pliers so it is centered on the wire.

OPENING JUMP RINGS AND LINKS Always open jump rings and links sideways, using hard-nose pliers. Opening them otherwise will weaken the wire and cause the circle to lose its integrity.

WRAPPED WIRE LINKS Place round-nose pliers about $\frac{1}{2}$ inch from the end of the wire and curl. Wrap the wire around the pliers rather than trying to force it with the pliers. You should have a tail of about $\frac{1}{2}$ inch. The length will depend on the number of wraps you want to make. Straighten loop and tail so the loop is centered on the wire. Grab loop between hard-nose pliers and wind tail around the rest of the wire with your fingers. Snip off excess wire so that there are an equal number of wraps on each side.

1

necklaces

Knotted Sea Spray Pearls

Since pearls have retained their classic status, I feel I can let out a little secret—knotting pearls is easy. Once you get the hang of it, you can knot a fine strand on silk, using bead tips for a more finished look. When deciding on the length of any knotted necklace, always consider that each knot takes up about ½ inch of thread. So, for an 18-inch knotted necklace, you'll need double the length of thread (36 inches).

YOU WILL NEED:

1 yard pale green embroidery thread

1 yard pale blue embroidery thread

2 sterling rings

Thirty 8mm freshwater pearls

Tweezers

Glue, nail polish, or bead cement

S-clasp

1. Tie one end of green thread and one end of blue thread onto one ring.

2. Starting with the green thread, tie a knot 1 inch down from the ring. (Always make sure your knots are small and tight, to avoid stretch and tension on the thread.) String a pearl onto the thread and pull it up flush against the knot. Next, tie a very loose knot. Bring the knot close to the pearl by placing tweezers through the loose knot and grabbing the thread very close to the pearl (see page 15 for more on knotting with tweezers). Pull the thread taut. Continue in the same manner, spacing the pearls as desired. Consider spacing them randomly for a unique look. Repeat, knotting and stringing pearls on the blue thread.

3. When you have finished knotting both threads, tie both ends to the other ring, as in step 1. Drop a bead of glue only on the knots around the rings. Slip the S-clasp into the rings.

In Cursive Necklace

Say it without words. This scribble is plenty decipherable as a good gift, and the quick-and-easy stitch is fun to experiment with. Try making matching earrings or bracelets. You can make this necklace so that the loops graduate in size, or just keep each loop the same.

YOU WILL NEED:

Twisted wire needle

2 yards "D"-size nylon thread

2 steel or silver end rings (jump or

split)

Glue, nail polish, or bead cement

1 strand "silver" glass seed beads

S-clasp

1. Thread the needle with nylon thread and knot ends together. Tie an end ring to the thread end. Glue knot and cut ends when dry.

2. String about 3 inches of seed beads.

3. To make the first loop, string eight seed beads. Take needle back through the first bead in that sequence and exit this same bead. Pull taut to form a loop.

4. String another sequence, this time of nine beads. Repeat step 2 to make a second loop. If you want the loops to graduate in size, increase the number of seed beads in each loop by twos. (For instance, make the second loop with a sequence of ten beads instead of eight.) After the center loop is made, decrease the number of beads in each loop by two for a symmetrical graduation.

5. Continue adding loops, with nine beads between loops. When you have made your last loop, finish with 3 inches of beads.

6. Take needle through an end ring. Make a knot, glue, and snip ends when dry.

7. Slip the S-clasp into the end rings.

Peyote Button Necklace

The peyote stitch looks and sounds more complicated than it is. Once you get the hang of the stitch, you might try making a double-stranded necklace, using contrasting colors of beads.

1. Thread the needle with nylon thread and knot ends together. String on a bead tip, making sure the hook faces out and that the tip doesn't slip over the knot. String seed beads until you come to the center of your necklace, about 8 to 10 inches of beads.

2. String twenty to twenty-five more seed beads. Curl these beads into a loop, bringing the loop close to the rest of the strung beads. Tie knot snugly between the loop and the other beads.

3. Take your needle through the first bead in the loop, add a bead, and take it through the third bead in the loop. Continue in this fashion, adding a bead before taking your needle through every other bead in the loop. When you have completed the loop, take your needle through the last seed bead so that it is headed in the opposite direction from which it came. Finish stringing the rest of the seed beads as in step 1.

4. Add the remaining bead tip after the last bead. Tie a loose knot, pulling it down into the bead tip using tweezers or hard-nose pliers. To do this, insert the tweezers through the loop, and grab onto the thread coming out of the bead tip (see page 15 for more on knotting inside a bead tip). Glue all knots and snip ends when dry. Hook the clasp loops to the ends of the bead tips and close the bead tip loops using hard-nose pliers.

Floating Pearl Necklace

It's easy to make magic. Float pearls in their own orbit using coated nylon wire and crimps. You can substitute any kind of beads for the pearls.

YOU WILL NEED:

28 sterling crimp beads

18 to 20 inches coated wire

2 split rings

Hard-nose pliers

7 grey freshwater pearls

6 pink freshwater pearls

Clasp

1. String a crimp bead on one end of the wire and take the wire through a split ring. Take wire back through crimp bead, pull tight, and smash the crimp using hard-nose pliers (see page 15 for more on crimping). Snip excess tails.

2. String on another crimp bead. Using hard-nose pliers, smash the bead about 1 inch away from the split ring. String on a grey pearl, followed by another crimp bead. Smash the crimp on the other side of the pearl. Continue to string crimps and alternating colors of pearls.

3. When you come to the end of your necklace, string a final crimp bead and take wire through the second split ring. Pull tightly so that the wire loop is small. Take wire back though crimp bead and smash crimp. Snip excess tail.

4. Add the clasp (see page 15 for more on adding a clasp).

Charming Charm Necklace

With a stack of headpins, you can turn your favorite beads into charms. If you want to give your necklace an "antique" look, you can oxidize the chain using a product called Silver-Black. Brush it on with an old paintbrush, then rinse it in water. When dry, use steel wool to brush the chain.

YOU WILL NEED:

9 beads of varying color (Austrian
    crystal, amethyst, amber, or peridot,
    or 9 pre-made silver charms on jump
    rings)

Bali daisy spacers (optional)

Up to 9 headpins

Round-nose pliers

Nippers

16 to 20 inches sterling chain

Hard-nose pliers

Jump rings (optional)

Toggle clasp

1. To make beads into charms, string a bead, or a bead and a Bali spacer, onto a headpin and make a single loop at the top using round-nose pliers (see page 16 for more on making charms). Using nippers, snip off excess wire.

2. Use nippers to cut a piece of chain about ½ inch long. Cut one link of the chain at its seam. Open link to the side using hard-nose pliers (see page 17 for more on opening links). Close this link around a link at the center of the long piece of chain; your central component will hang from this chain.

3. Begin adding the headpins or charms on the links of the long chain. Do this by opening the wire loops on the charms, hanging them on the chain, and closing them using hard-nose pliers. If the charms are not hanging correctly, you may have to add jump rings to get charms to hang straight. Select and hang a charm from the short piece of chain.

4. Add the clasp to the chain ends by opening the end links of the chain using nippers, slipping on the clasp, and closing the link using hard-nose pliers.

Note: To make a side-drilled bead into a charm, see Amber Drop Earrings (page 83).

Flower Garden Necklace

This piece makes a showcase of chaos. It seems each alternating bead is different. Usually it is best for beginners to keep the degree of variance in a piece to a minimum. But in this necklace almost all the beads are somewhat flat and flowerlike, so they do not compete with each other. The flower beads used here have loops for petals, forming natural links for the necklace.

Nippers

18- or 20-gauge sterling wire

Round-nose pliers

Pen

2 end rings (jump or split)

Hard-nose pliers

14 assorted silver beads

14 assorted silver flower beads

S-clasp

1. Using nippers, cut 1 inch of sterling wire. Grasp one end of the wire using round-nose pliers and curl the wire around the tip of the pliers to form a loop (see page 16 for more on making a wire loop). Remember where exactly on the pliers you placed the wire; this will help you to make each loop uniform. You may even want to mark the pliers with a pen. Before closing the loop, add an end ring, then use hard-nose pliers to close the loop.

2. Thread a silver bead onto the wire. Use round-nose pliers to curl a loop on the other end of the bead. Attach loop to a petal on a flower bead.

3. Cut another piece of wire, make a loop, and attach it to a petal on the other side of flower bead. Now close the loop using hard-nose pliers, add a silver bead, and make a loop on the other side. Continue adding links, alternating beads and flower beads, until you have reached the desired length, attaching the remaining end ring to the last loop of the last link. Slip the S-clasp through the end rings.

Little Breeze Necklace

This double-stranded necklace is made up of wire loop links, and thus it will take a little more time than most projects in this book. The process will go more quickly if you lay out all your beads first in your desired sequence. To speed things up even further, you can pre-cut the wire for the links, once you figure out how much each bead requires.

YOU WILL NEED:

Nippers

22-gauge steel wire

Round-nose pliers

Pen

2 end rings (jump or split)

Hard-nose pliers

12 to 15 assorted beads, such as baby-blue
    Czech faceted glass beads, Indian silver
    beads

¹⁄₂ strand Bali or Indian daisy spacers

2 large Indian silver rings

S-clasp

1. Using nippers, cut 1 inch of the 22-gauge wire. Grasp one end of the wire using your round-nose pliers and curl the wire around the tip of the pliers to form a loop (see page 16 for more on making a wire loop). Remember where exactly on the pliers you placed the wire; this will help you to make each loop uniform. You may even want to mark the pliers with a pen. Before closing the loop, add an end ring, then use hard-nose pliers to close the loop.

2. Thread a bead onto the wire. Use round-nose pliers to curl a loop on the other end of the bead.

3. Using nippers, cut another inch of the 22-gauge wire. Curl one end of the wire into a loop as directed in step 1. Before closing the loop, attach it to the loop in the first link. Close the loop. Thread a daisy onto the wire and use round-nose pliers to curl a loop on the other end of the daisy. Continue adding links in this manner, alternating beads with daisies in any sequence you like, until you have approximately 4 inches of links. Onto the last loop of this length, attach the large silver ring.

4. The single strand necklace will now become a double strand necklace as you begin two new, separate lengths on the silver spacer. To create these lengths, begin as you did in step one, attaching a wire loop to the spacer. Thread a bead or daisy onto this wire,

curling a loop at the other end of the bead. Continue making lengths until you have approximately 5 inches of links. Begin again at the same silver spacer, making a second length of links slightly longer than the first—one or two links longer. Attach the ends of these two new lengths to a second large silver ring.

5. Finish the necklace by making a final length of links identical to the first, 4-inch series of links that you made. At the end of this length, attach the wire loop to an end ring. Slip the S-clasp through the end rings.

Stick Chain Necklace

It is actually quite easy to make your own chain. For this particular design, you can hammer the wire so that it has flat sides, or just leave it round. Either way, make sure the wire will fit through the spacer beads that you have chosen before you begin. Variance in the lengths of chain adds to the charm of the piece.

YOU WILL NEED:

Nippers

18-gauge sterling wire

Chasing hammer and steel plate or thin
    cotton cloth (optional)

Steel wool (optional)

Round-nose pliers

Hard-nose pliers

23 assorted Ball or Indian spacers

Clasp

1. Using nippers, cut 22 pieces of wire, each between $1/2$ and 1 inch long. If desired, hammer pieces flat on a steel plate or on a thin cotton cloth laid flat over a concrete surface (such as a sidewalk). If desired, use steel wool to bring shine back to hammered pieces.

2. Curl ends of wire pieces into loops using round-nose pliers, keeping the loops uniform in size and direction (see page 16 for more on making wire loops).

3. Lay out wire pieces in any order you like. Starting from one end, open one loop using hard-nose pliers and attach a spacer bead. Open the other side using hard-nose pliers and add another spacer. Close the loop. This is the first link of the chain.

4. Take the second piece of wire, open one loop and attach it to a spacer in the first link. Continue adding links in this fashion. Attach the clasp in the same way, using small wire pieces to link the end spacers to each side of the clasp.

River-to-River Necklace

The key to this necklace is fluidity. Using different styles of chain could cause chaos. For continuity's sake, make sure one section of chain is the same on the top as on the bottom. A bead cap or decorative bead serves as a link between the chains.

YOU WILL NEED:

Nippers

15 inches chain

20- or 22-gauge wire

Round-nose pliers

7 ½ inches filagree chain, or other
    decorative chain

Hard-nose pliers

2 bead caps

Lobster clasp

Jump or split ring

1. Using nippers, cut the 15-inch chain into 3 sections: 7 inches, 4 inches, and 4 inches. Set these last two sections aside.

2. Cut a section of wire a little less than 1 inch. Make a loop using round-nose pliers, leaving a tail of about ¼ inch. Bring the tail straight up so that both wires are parallel. Thread the ends of the 7- and 7½ -inch sections of chain onto the loop, and pinch the loop closed using hard-nose pliers. Place a bead cap over both wires. Make sure the loop is small enough so that the bead cap will cover it.

3. On the top of the bead cap make a loop, leaving a tail of about ¼ inch. Thread the end of a 4-inch section of chain onto the loop and close the loop. Wrap the tail around twice. Snip excess tail.

4. Repeat step 2, threading the loose ends of the 7- and 7 ½-inch sections of chain onto the wire loop and adding the second bead cap. Repeat step 3, threading the end of the remaining section of 4-inch chain onto the loop.

5. Add the lobster clasp to the two 4-inch chain ends with the jump ring or split ring (see page 15 for more on adding a clasp).

Bella Bola Tie Necklace

Crimp findings have a crimp at one end and a loop at the other. They are traditionally crimped to the ends of thread or wire and then attached to a clasp. In this project, they function as pendant hangers. The slider bead serves as a decoration as well as a means to adjust the necklace. In choosing your snake chain and slider bead, be sure the chain fits snugly through the holes in the bead with some resistance.

YOU WILL NEED:

Snake chain, any width

Nippers

1 flat, 2-holed slider bead

2 crimp findings

Hard-nose pliers

2 pendants

Jump or split rings (optional)

1. Measure enough snake chain to slip over your head easily, and cut using nippers.

2. String both ends of chain through the slider bead.

3. Slip the crimp end of a crimp finding over one end of the snake chain and smash crimp using pliers. Repeat with the remaining crimp finding and the other end of snake chain.

4. Add the two pendants onto the loops of the crimp findings using jump rings or split rings to attach, if necessary.

Waterfall Necklace

The glints in this crystal necklace are second only to sun on water. This particularly quick and easy project involves simple knotting and gluing. Try varying the length of the necklace, or making an additional strand to wear simultaneously.

YOU WILL NEED:

24 small vermeil daisies, assorted shapes

12 assorted beads such as crystal balls or
    quartz beads

2 crimp beads

18 to 20 inches nylon filament

2 split rings

Hard-nose pliers

Glue, nail polish, or bead cement

Clasp

1. Lay out your beads in the desired sequence.

2. String a crimp bead on one end of nylon filament and take the filament through a split ring. Take filament back through crimp, pull tight, and smash crimp using hard-nose pliers.

3. About an inch down from the loop, add a daisy and tie a knot. Place a drop of glue on the knot and slide a crystal ball or quartz bead over the glued knot. Add another daisy and place small drops of glue on the outside of both daisies. The glue will dry clear, holding the daisies and crystal ball in place.

4. Continue to thread daisies and beads, knot, and glue as desired. Make longer clusters of crystal balls, quartz beads, and daisies, or let a crystal ball or quartz bead stand alone.

5. Stop your bead sequence $1\frac{1}{2}$ inches from the end of the filament. String a crimp bead on the end and take the filament through a split ring. Take filament back through crimp, pull tight, and smash crimp using hard-nose pliers. Snip excess tails.

6. Add the clasp (see page 15 for more on adding a clasp).

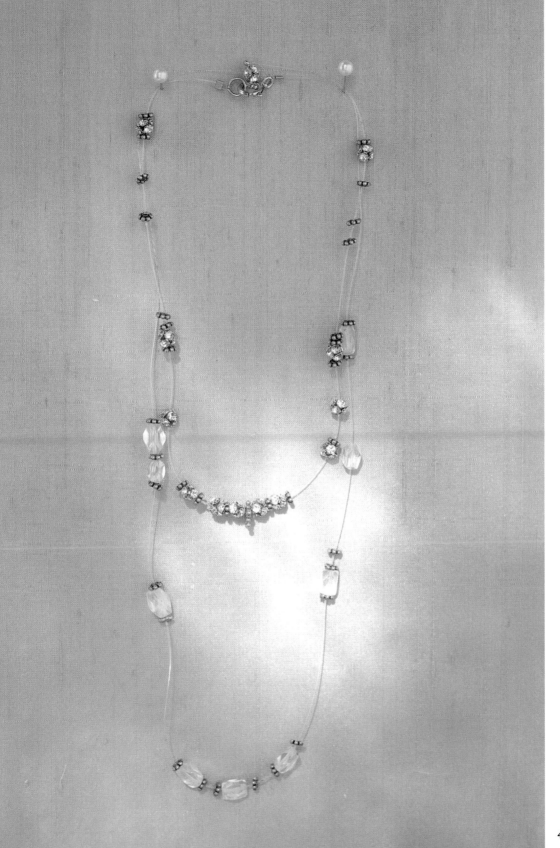

Lariat Necklace

Coated wire is perfect for hanging heavy beads; look for flexible wire with many strands. You can wear this necklace as a lariat by loosely tying one end over the other. Add the optional S-clasp for two looks: a long, single-stranded necklace, or wrap it around twice for a shorter double-stranded version.

YOU WILL NEED:

Nippers

Coated wire

2 crimp beads

2 end rings

Hard-nose pliers

15 large Czech red glass beads

60 assorted small beads such as

    Czech glass cuts and African

    aluminum or nickel beads

S-clasp (optional)

1. Using nippers, cut just over 1 yard of coated wire, or cut a piece long enough so that the necklace will fit easily over your head. String a crimp bead on one end, followed by an end ring. Take the wire back through the crimp bead, pull tight, and smash the crimp bead flat using hard-nose pliers. Begin stringing beads in any order you like.

2. When you come to the end of your necklace, string the remaining crimp bead and end ring. Again, take the wire back through the crimp, pull tight so that there is no slack between the ring and the last bead, then smash the crimp bead. Hide the tail end through the last bead. Add S-clasp, if desired.

chokers

2

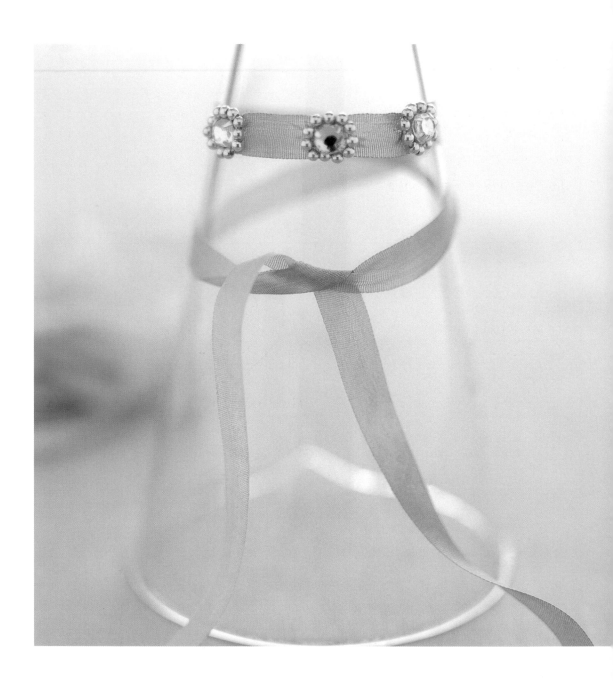

Forget-Me-Not Choker

Ribbon jewelry can be as delicate as lingerie—you won't be overlooked in this sweet little number. Tie this pretty choker in the back, or add beads on the ends and wear the bow in front. Sew-on rhinestones are flat-backed and four-holed, so they're easy to stitch; you can find them in any craft or fabric store.

Size 10 needle

18 inches white nylon thread

18 to 20 inches ribbon

3 sew-on rhinestones

Thirty-three 1mm sterling balls

Glue, nail polish, or bead cement

1. Thread the needle with nylon thread. Find the center of the ribbon and stitch rhinestones to the ribbon, taking the needle through it at least twice at each hole to secure. Knot and clip thread ends at the back of the ribbon.

2. Beside the rhinestone, take the needle up through the ribbon from the back side and string on three of the sterling balls. Secure the balls along the curve of the rhinestone by inserting the needle back through the ribbon close to the rhinestone and pulling taut.

3. Take the needle back again through these same three balls (to reinforce the first). The thread should enter from the first ball and exit from the third.

4. String three more balls and repeat steps 2 and 3, following the curve of the rhinestone. Repeat again with three more balls. Complete the frame of balls around the rhinestone by repeating steps 2 and 3 with just two balls. Glue all your knots, and snip when dry.

5. Repeat steps 2, 3, and 4 to add two more rhinestones, one on each side of the first.

Rope and Joy Choker

The large bead works like a button—just pop it through the beaded loop on the other end. Try using contrasting colors of cord and bead for different effects. Look for a needle strong enough to pierce the cord, yet thin enough to accommodate the beads; otherwise you will need to use two needles and switch in the middle of sewing.

YOU WILL NEED:

13 to 16 inches silk cord, depending on
    neck size

Glue, nail polish, or bead cement

Needle

Elastic thread

One 8mm bead

Ten 1mm beads

1. Apply drops of glue to the ends of the cord to prevent fraying, and let dry.

2. Thread the needle and make a stitch about ¼ inch in from one end of cord. Wrap elastic once around the cord. Make another stitch next to the first. Continue wrapping and stitching, moving closer to the end of the cord. Reinforce the end with stitches on either side of the cord, then thread on the large bead.

3. Take the needle back up through the cord, making sure the bead is centered. You can take the thread back through the bead a second time if the hole is big enough. Knot thread close to the cord, glue, and snip when dry.

4. Stitch and wrap the other end of the cord in exactly the same way. When you get to the end, thread the small beads and make a loop, taking your needle back through the opposite side of the cord. Take the needle back up through the cord. Stitch for reinforcement. Knot, glue, and snip when dry.

Shady Evening Choker

Elastic thread makes this choker easy to slip on and slip off. Once you get the hang of the simple "stitch," you can experiment with color. Try using two intensities of purple, adding a darker or lighter shade when you get to the center of the choker—the finished choker will appear to graduate in color. You can also use two completely different colors for a sharp contrast.

YOU WILL NEED:

Twisted wire needle

3 yards elastic thread

2 strands faceted Czech purple 4mm
    glass beads

Glue, nail polish, or bead cement

Nippers

1. Thread the needle with the elastic thread. Tie a knot next to the needle rather than doubling the thread. This will prevent your thread from slipping out of the needle. String six beads and bring beads down to end of thread. Curl the string of beads into a loop, and tie the thread tail to the thread, just above the last bead, securing the loop. You'll see that the beads form a sort of oval, with two beads each on the two sides, and one bead each on the top and bottom. The knot should be just to the side of the top bead.

2. String five beads and take needle back through the *first* bead you strung (the bead at the top of the first loop). Your needle should exit the bead at the knot.

3. Now take the needle back through the seventh and eighth beads you strung (the two beads on the side of the new loop). This is so you can begin again at the top of the new loop. String five more beads, and repeat steps 2 and 3. Continue to add five beads for each stitch, taking the needle back through the top of the previous rectangle, and then through the side of the current oval.

4. When you have enough loops to reach your desired length—approximately 38 loops—you will need to join the ends. To do this, string two beads and take the needle through the top bead of the very first oval, String two more beads, take the needle back up through the bottom bead of the last rectangle, forming a final rectangle which joins the first and last together. Knot, glue, and snip ends with nippers when dry.

Cleopatra Choker

Whip up something today that you can wear tonight. Memory wire is pre-shaped for necklaces, bracelets, and rings. "Memory wire" holds its shape, making clasps optional. When constructing a design for memory wire, it is a good idea to experiment with the bead sequence on a beading board or towel rather than taking beads on and off the wire. Try varying the colors as well as the patterns.

YOU WILL NEED:

18 inches necklace memory wire

Round-nose pliers

Hard-nose pliers

1 strand blue African glass beads

2 vermeil daisy spacers

1 faceted burgundy bead

Charms (optional)

1. Make a loop in one end of the wire using round-nose pliers. To make the loop, grab one end of the wire and grip tightly. Force the wire around the curve of the pliers, then straighten the loop using hard-nose pliers.

2. String African glass beads until you reach the center of your choker. String a vermiel spacer, the burgundy bead, and another spacer. Fill the memory wire with the remaining glass beads. Make a loop at the end of the wire as in step 1. Although you won't need a clasp, you may decide to add decorative charms to the loops on the ends.

Barn Dance Choker

It is helpful to use multiple-holed spacer bars if you want to stack more than one strand of memory wire; otherwise you may have trouble getting the strands to lie correctly. In this case I have used a decorative triple-holed clasp (which doubles as a centerpiece) to keep each strand separate.

YOU WILL NEED:

Nippers

1²/₃ yards necklace memory wire

Round-nose pliers

Hard-nose pliers

One 3-stranded clasp

3 strands Czech glass beads

1. Using nippers, cut three different sections of memory wire. The smallest should be approximately 18 inches long, the next 19 inches long, and the third 20 inches long, depending on your neck size. When measuring your neck, add 1 inch to the wire length for the clasp loops.

2. Beginning with the shortest length of wire, make a loop in one end using round-nose pliers. To make the loop, grab one end of the wire and grip tightly. Force the wire around the curve of the pliers, then straighten the loop using hard-nose pliers. Attach the loop to the *topmost* hole on one side of the clasp and close the loop using hard-nose pliers.

3. String on the beads, filling the length of the wire, and make a loop at the other end. Before closing, attach it to the topmost loop of the other side of the clasp.

4. Repeat steps 2 and 3 with the second-longest section of wire, attaching the ends to the middle loops of the clasp. Repeat again with the longest section of wire, attaching each end to the last loop on either side of the clasp.

Cocktail Choker

This double-stranded necklace takes its inspiration from Native American chokers. Instead of bone and leather spacers, I have used garnet beads and star spacers for a more modern look. The star spacers are large enough to accommodate both strands of the necklace, holding them together and ensuring that the necklace lies properly.

YOU WILL NEED:

Nippers

1 yard coated wire

4 crimp beads

2-stranded clasp

Hard-nose pliers

1 strand faceted garnets

40 small daisy spacers

1 strand glass bugles

5 large star spacers

S-clasp

1. Using nippers, cut two 18-inch strands of coated wire and set one aside. String a crimp bead on one end and take the wire through one loop in a two-stranded clasp. Take wire back through crimp bead, pull tight, and smash the crimp using hard-nose pliers (see page 15 for more on crimping).

2. String on the bead sequence garnet-daisy-bugle-daisy-garnet-daisy, or any desired variation on this sequence. String on a large star spacer.

3. String the above bead sequence, this time twice. Add another large star spacer.

4. Repeat step 3 three more times. After the last star spacer, finish with the sequence garnet-daisy-bugle-daisy-garnet. String a crimp bead on the end and take the wire through one loop in the other side of the two-stranded clasp and back through crimp. Pull tightly to take up slack and smash crimp. Snip tail or stick it back through the last bead in the sequence.

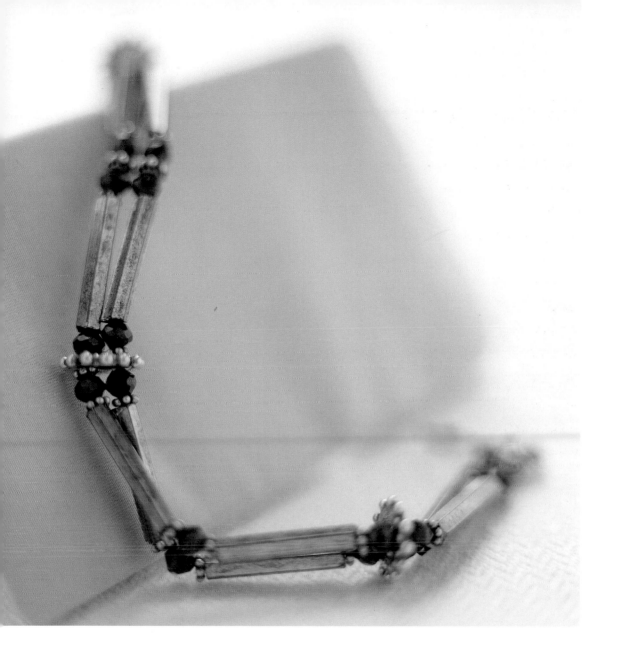

5. String the second strand just as you did the first. Begin by crimping one end through the second loop in the two-stranded clasp, and string the sequence as in step 2. Instead of stringing on a large star spacer, join the second strand with the first by taking the wire through the star spacer in the first strand. Continue stringing the sequence and joining the second strand to the first through each large spacer bead until you've finished. Crimp end and attach to clasp as you did in step 4.

Chainges Choker

You can use any type of chain for this project; just make sure the links are generous enough to accomodate the wire.

YOU WILL NEED:

Nippers

10 inches chain

6½ inches chain, slightly lighter

4 inches 24-gauge steel wire

Round-nose pliers

Hard-nose pliers

4 bead caps

4 pink freshwater pearls

Clasp

1. Using nippers, cut the 10-inch length of chain into two 5-inch lengths. Cut the 6½-inch length of chain into two lengths, one 3 inches and one 3½ inches.

2. Cut 4 sections of wire each a little less than 1 inch long. Make a loop in one using round-nose pliers (see page 16 for more on making wire loops). Before closing the loop completely, thread on both segments of the lighter chain. Close the loop using hard-nose pliers. Thread a bead cap and a pearl on the wire. Make a loop on the other side and thread on a 5-inch length of chain.

3. Make a loop in a second section of wire, thread on both free ends of the lighter chain. Close the loop. Thread a bead cap and a pearl on the wire. Make a loop on the other side and thread on the remaining 5-inch length of chain.

4. Make a loop in a third section of wire, threading one of the free ends of heavier chain. Close the loop. Thread a bead cap and a pearl on the wire. Make a loop on the other side.

5. Repeat step 4 with remaining section of wire, threading the first loop on the last free end of chain, adding remaining bead cap and pearl, finishing with a loop. Add the clasp (see page 15 for more on adding clasps).

3

bracelets

Garter Charm Bracelet

This fancy garterlike bracelet needs very little to recommend it—a few silver pendants add charm. Browse a good fabric store for pretty trimmings, sold by the yard. You can also make your own charms using beads and headpins (see page 16 for more on making charms).

YOU WILL NEED:

Trimming

Size 10 beading needle

Nylon thread

2 large end rings (jump or split)

1 jump ring

Hard-nose pliers

3 charms

S-clasp

1. Measure and cut a length of trimming to fit your wrist.

2. Thread the needle. Slip the end of trimming into an end ring, fold over ¼ inch and stitch down. Knot thread and clip ends. Repeat on other side of trimming.

3. Open the jump ring sideways using the pliers (see page 12 for more on opening jump rings). At the center of the bracelet, slip the jump ring onto the edge of the trimming (or stitch it on) and through the loops in the three charms. Close the jump ring.

4. Slip the S-clasp through the end rings.

Cross-My-Heart Bracelet

Because memory wire retains or "remembers" its shape, you might find yourself wrestling with it if you don't plan your design carefully. This is one of those times a beading board is really helpful; rather than taking beads on and off the wire, lay out your beads on a board or towel.

YOU WILL NEED:

Assorted beads such as glass bicones, seed
   beads, and/or faceted glass beads

Nippers

Bracelet memory wire

Round-nose pliers

Hard-nose pliers

2 heart charms

1. Measure your wrist size adding 3 to 4 inches to the length for crossover plus $\frac{1}{2}$ inch for the end loops. Lay out your desired sequence of beads. Using nippers, cut a length of memory wire.

2. Make a loop in one end of the wire using round-nose pliers. To make the loop, grab one end of the wire and grip tightly. Force the wire around the curve of the pliers, then straighten the loop using hard-nose pliers. Before closing, add a heart charm.

3. String on the desired sequence of beads and make a loop at the other end of the memory wire; add the second heart charm and close. Memory wire will keep its shape, and you don't need a clasp.

Claspless Button Bracelet

This bracelet depends on tension; the looped end will fit securely around the button only by making careful wrist measurements.

YOU WILL NEED:

2 crystal drops

2 headpins

Round-nose pliers

Nippers

1 inch 20- to 22-gauge wire

1 button

Nylon wire

2 crimp beads

Hard-nose pliers

1 strand AB or Iris seed beads

1. Thread a crystal drop onto a headpin and make a loop at the top using round-nose pliers. Repeat with the other crystal and headpin. Set charms aside.

2. Using nippers, cut 1 inch of wire and thread each end through a buttonhole. Turn the button over and curl each wire end into a small loop. Each loop should be small enough that a seed bead will not slip through it. Set aside.

3. Measure your wrist and cut double the length of nylon wire, plus 3 inches. String a crimp bead on one end. Take the wire through the loop, one crystal charm, and back through crimp bead. Smash the crimp using hard-nose pliers.

4. String 1 inch of seed beads onto the nylon wire and thread one wire loop of the button onto the wire. Continue adding seed beads until you are about 2 inches from the end of the wire. Thread wire through other loop in button and add another inch of seed beads. Crimp end and add remaining charm as in step 3. Cut tail ends using nippers.

5. To fasten, lay the button end of the bracelet on your wrist and wrap the bracelet around your wrist, pulling the loop over the button.

Snake-Wrap Bracelet

This bracelet is inspired by Ethiopian ankle cuffs. You can find inspiration for new designs everywhere—thrift stores, flea markets, and old National Geographic magazines are all good sources for ideas.

Nippers

18-gauge sterling wire

Hard-nose pliers

2 Indian silver "cut" beads

2 Indian silver flower beads or spacers

1 yard 22-gauge sterling wire

Assorted Bali sliders

1. Measure your wrist and, using nippers, cut a section of the 18-gauge wire to fit, subtracting 1 inch for the space between the ends. Bend this section of wire around your wrist to shape it. Your wrist should just slip through the space between the ends.

2. Use hard-nose pliers to make a tiny fold in one end of the wire. Thread a silver cut and an Indian flower bead or spacer onto the wire from the opposite end. The wire fold should prevent the bead from slipping off the bracelet.

3. Cut 1 yard of the 22-gauge wire and begin wrapping it around the 18-gauge wire, starting at the flower bead and moving out. Keep wires coiled tight and close together, using hard-nose pliers if necessary. Stop wrapping 1 inch from the end. Add Bali sliders or spacers large enough to fit easily over the coiled wire. Thread on the remaining Indian flower bead or spacer and silver cut. Fold the end over using hard-nose pliers.

4. Continue wrapping wire, pushing the flower and cut bead flush to the folded end. Snip excess wire.

Baby's Breath Bracelet

This delicate bracelet makes a perfect shower gift. It is made up of a series of wrapped wire links. It's a bit tricky the first time, but it gets easier with practice. You can start out making bigger wire links on steel to master the technique. The extension chain allows for the baby's wrist to grow—the length of the bracelet is adjustable.

YOU WILL NEED:

Nippers

22- or 24-gauge gold-fill wire

Round-nose pliers

1 to 2 inches gold-fill extension chain

Hard-nose pliers

12 assorted beads, such as Austrian
    crystal beads, freshwater pearls, and
    tourmaline drops

Gold clasp

1. Using nippers, cut 1 inch of the gold-fill wire. Curl one end into a loop using round-nose pliers, leaving a short tail. Slip the last link of the extension chain onto the loop, grasp the loop firmly using hard-nose pliers, and wrap the wire tail around the base of the loop at least twice (see page 17 for more on wrapped wire links). Snip away any extra wire.

2. Add a crystal bead and make a loop on the other side of the wire, leaving the same length of tail. Wrap tail as in step 1.

3. Cut another inch of wire and curl one end into a loop using round-nose pliers, leaving a short tail. Before closing, slip the end of the link you just made onto the loop. Grasp loop firmly using hard-nose pliers and wrap the tail as in step 1.

4. Repeat step 2, this time adding a pearl. Repeat again using a tourmaline drop. Continue to make links in this manner until you reach the desired length.

5. Attach the clasp to the end (see page 15 for more on adding a clasp).

White Light Anklet

There are a wide variety of decorative findings that just snap or crimp on, making it easy to change the charm or pendant on the snake chain at a whim.

YOU WILL NEED:

Snake chain, any width

Nippers

Crimp hook-and-eye clasp

Hard-nose pliers

Assorted beads such as Bali star spacers,
**   Thai cuts, assorted charms**

Sterling crimp beads (optional)

Headpins (optional)

Round-nose pliers (optional)

1. Measure your ankle and subtract about ½ inch from your measurement, as the length of the clasp will add approximately ½ inch. Cut the appropriate length of chain, using nippers.

2. Slip one side of the crimp clasp over one end and smash crimp using hard-nose pliers.

3. String beads onto the chain to let them free float. Alternatively, if you want the beads to stay in place, precede each bead with a crimp bead and follow it with a second crimp. Position the bead where you want it to be on the anklet, and smash the crimps using hard-nose pliers on either end to hold the bead in place.

4. If desired, add a central charm or two. Make your own by stringing a bead onto a headpin and curling the end of the headpin into a loop using round-nose pliers (see page 16 for more on making charms). You can make an assortment of charms in this manner. If you want to make them interchangeable, remember to make the loops in the headpins large enough that the pendant can be slipped over the beads of the anklet as well as the clasp.

5. Slip the other side of the crimp clasp over the end of the chain and smash the crimp using hard-nose pliers.

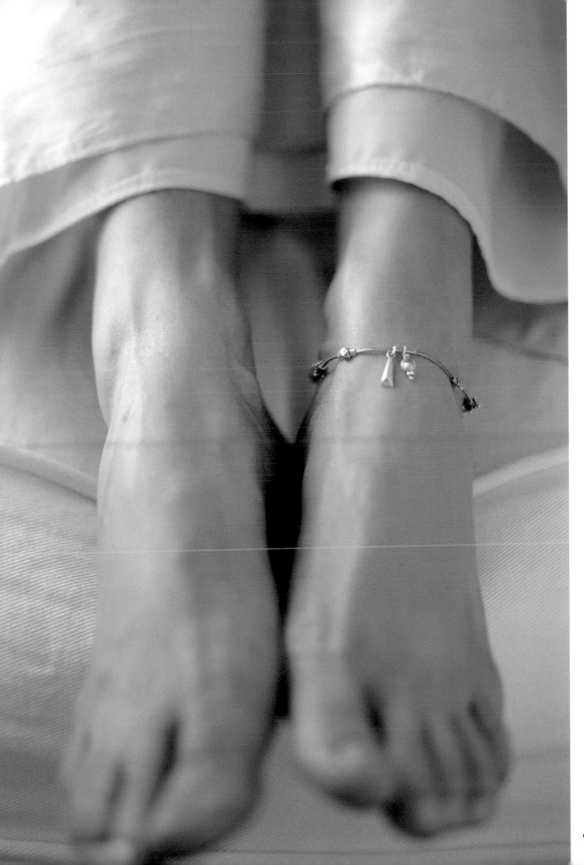

earrings

Flower Stitch Earrings

You will be the prize stem in these easy-stitch earrings. Try hanging them as charms or pendants too.

YOU WILL NEED:

16 inches "D" nylon

Twisted wire needle

Eighteen 1mm Czech "bronze" faceted
   glass beads

2 Czech faceted glass barrels

2 gold-fill posts or French hooks

2 gold-fill bead tips (optional)

Round-nosed pliers (optional)

Glue, nail polish, or bead cement

1. Thread a twisted wire needle.

2. String nine "bronze" glass beads, then tie the ends together, forming a circle.

3. Take the needle through all nine beads again, thread on a glass barrel, then take needle back up through the last five beads. Now tie the ends together.

4. String the ends through the loop in the ear post or hook, and tie a knot. Or, thread the ends through a bead tip, and tie a knot inside the bead tip using pliers (see page 15 for more information on knotting inside a bead tip). Glue, clip tails when dry.

5. Repeat these steps for other earring.

Eclipse Earrings

These circles of silver beads are very simple to put together. While no one can deny the elegance of silver, you can use any kind of bead to make these little hanging hoops.

YOU WILL NEED:

Nippers

8 inches coated nylon wire

4 crimp beads

Hard-nose pliers

22 assorted silver beads

2 kidney wires or other earring findings

1. Using nippers, cut the wire in half. Take the end of one wire length through a crimp bead. Take that same end back through the crimp in the opposite direction, forming a small loop. Using hard-nose pliers, smash the crimp.

2. String half the silver beads onto the wire in any order you like. String on another crimp bead. Take the wire end through the wire loop on the other end, and back through the crimp, pulling the wire to make a small loop the same size as the first. Smash the crimp bead. Snip excess wire tails.

3. Repeat these steps for the second hoop. Slip the hoops onto the kidney wires.

Bridesmaid Earrings

These pretty earrings are very simple to make. Maybe "always a bridesmaid, never a bride" is a good thing. You can find headpins with decorative heads for added flair.

YOU WILL NEED:

2 Bali star spacers

2 Austrian crystal beads

2 bead caps

2 headpins

Round-nose pliers

Hard-nose pliers

Nippers

2 French hooks or ear wires

1. String a Bali star, a crystal, and a bead cap onto a headpin.

2. Make a loop next to the bead cap using round-nose pliers, leaving a tail of $\frac{1}{2}$ inch. Straighten loop using hard-nose pliers, then bring tail twice around neck of loop. You can do this by holding the loop flat between hard-nose pliers and pulling wire around with your fingers. Snip off excess wire using nippers. This process is identical to that of making a charm (see page 16 for more on making charms).

3. Open the loop of the French hook or ear wire sideways using hard-nose pliers. Add the looped headpin to the ear-wire loop and close.

4. Repeat these steps for other earring.

Amber Drop Earrings

The side-drilled beads used in this project are made to lie flat. With wire and round-nose pliers, you can manipulate any bead so that it will face the correct direction. Use this same technique to turn side drilled beads into charms.

YOU WILL NEED:

Nippers

3 inches 22- or 24-gauge gold-fill wire

2 amber teardrop beads

Round-nose pliers

2 French hooks or ear wires

Hard-nose pliers

1. Using nippers, cut 1½ inches of the gold-fill wire. Thread wire through a bead, bringing both ends up on either side of the bead. Cross the wires. Using round-nose pliers, make a double loop on one end. This loop should sit directly on top of drop. (Remember where you placed your pliers so that loops on other earring will be the same size.)

2. Take the other end of the wire and make a few wraps so that they sit directly under the loops. Snip off excess wire.

3. Open the loop of the French hook to the side using hard-nose pliers. Add the loop of the amber drop and close.

4. Repeat these steps for other earring.

After Midnight Earrings

Wear these earrings into the wee hours. Crystal teardrop beads have holes drilled sideways through their tops, making them the ideal bead for delicate drop earrings.

YOU WILL NEED:

Hard-nose pliers

2 large jump rings

2 crystal drop beads

Nippers

18-gauge wire

Round-nose pliers

2 vermeil beads

2 French hooks or ear wires

1. Using the hard-nose pliers, gently open a jump ring. Slip one end of the jump ring into one of the side holes in a drop bead. Gently close the jump ring, carefully pushing the other end of the jump ring into the other side hole in the drop bead. Gently pinch the jump ring so that ends of the ring touch inside the bead.

2. Using the nippers, cut 1 inch of the wire. Make a loop in one end using the round-nose pliers (see page 16 for more on making wire loops). Before closing, slip the drop bead jump ring onto the loop. Close the loop with hard-nose pliers.

3. Slip the vermeil bead onto the wire. Make a loop at the other end of the wire. Before closing, slip this loop through the loop in a French hook. Close the loop using hard-nose pliers.

4. Repeat these steps for other earring.

Removable Charm Earrings

These triangle hangers are great because they're easy to pry open, so charms are easily inter-changeable—new earrings without all the work! You can buy charms at the bead store, or make your own charms using beads and headpins (see page 16 for more on making charms).

YOU WILL NEED:

2 triangle hangers

Hard-nose pliers

2 charms

2 posts, ear wires, or hoops

2 jump rings (optional)

1. Open a triangle hanger sideways using hard-nose pliers. Slip a charm on the hanger and close the hanger.

2. Open the loop in the post or ear wire, or thread triangle directly onto a hoop. If the charm does not hang correctly, you can add a jump ring.

3. Repeat these steps for other earring.

Stick Chain Earrings

Showcase individual beads by dangling them from a length of wire. The wire can be hammered (see Stick Chain Necklace, page 35) or left round. Use vermeil post earring findings for a fancier earring—the decorative posts come with loops for attaching the dangling ear pendants.

YOU WILL NEED:

Nippers

2 inches 18-gauge gold-fill wire

   or 2 headpins

Round-nose pliers

Glue, nail polish, or bead cement

2 vermeil daisy spacers

2 burgundy citrine beads

2 vermeil posts with loop

Hard-nose pliers

1. Using the nippers, cut 1 inch of the gold-fill wire. Make a loop in one end using the round-nose pliers (see page 16 for more on making wire loops). At the other end add a drop of glue, then slide the daisy and citrine beads over it. This method is especially good for semi-precious stones, which can be drilled unevenly. If your beads are drilled evenly, you can slip them onto headpins, add the daisy spacer, make a loop at the top of the headpin, and proceed.

2. Open the loop of a post using hard-nose pliers and add citrine charm.

3. Repeat these steps for other earring.

Diamond Earrings

Okay, so they're not *real* diamonds, but some beaders find these silver Thai beads are the next best thing.

YOU WILL NEED:

Nippers

4 inches small oxidized sterling chain

3 inches 22- or 24-gauge steel wire
    or oxidized sterling wire

Round-nose pliers

2 Thai silver diamond beads

Hard-nose pliers

2 ball posts with loop

2 jump rings (optional)

1. Using nippers, cut chain into six pieces: two $1/2$-inch pieces, two $2/3$-inch pieces, and two $3/4$-inch pieces. Set aside.

2. Cut about $1 1/2$ inches of wire. Using round-nose pliers, make a tiny loop $1/2$ inch from one end. Bring the tail of the loop straight up so that both wire ends are parallel (one will be longer than the other). Thread on three different lengths of chain, $1/2$ inch, $2/3$ inch, $3/4$ inch.

3. Bring a diamond bead down over the wire ends.

4. Make a wire loop on top of the bead using round-nose pliers, leaving a tail of $1/2$ inch (see page 16 for more on making wire loops).

5. Straighten loop using hard-nose pliers, then bring tail once around neck of loop. Snip off excess wire. Open the loop of a ball post; add the looped diamond bead and close. If the bead is not hanging correctly from the post, use hard-nose pliers to change the direction of the loop, or add a jump ring.

6. Repeat these steps for other earring.

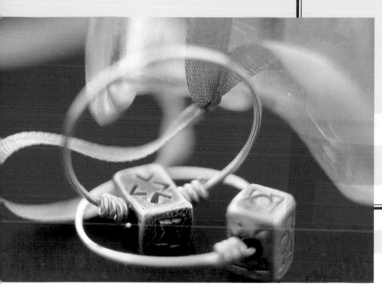

hair jewelry
and more

Cinderella Hair Band

Hair bands bring back childhood fantasies of fancy tiaras and gowns. You can use semi-precious beads such as garnets and freshwater pearls to set you a head above.

YOU WILL NEED:

3 yards elastic thread

2 twisted wire needles

1 strand freshwater pearls

1 strand faceted garnet beads

Glue, nail polish, or bead cement

Scissors

1. Thread each needle with a 1½-yard length of elastic thread. Do not double thread over. Knot one end of each thread, leaving a 2-inch tail.

2. String a pearl onto one needle and thread and pull it down to the knot. Take the second needle through the same pearl so the needles are pointed in opposite directions.

3. On one needle, thread a garnet and a pearl. On the second needle, thread a garnet, and take this needle through the pearl. Your needles should again be pointed in opposite directions. Repeat this stitch as many times as necessary for the desired length. Do not cut elastic ends.

4. For the underside of the hair band, string as many garnets onto elastic thread as necessary to fit the head comfortably. Subtract at least ½ inch to account for the stretch. Tie the ends of the thread to the hair band ends and knot securely. Glue knots and clip ends when dry.

Candy Store Clip

Turn any old grocery store clip into a keepsake. This is a great way to use a leftover assortment of beads. Pin curl clips have a nice flat surface for gluing beads. Different shades of one color lends unity to the jumble.

YOU WILL NEED:

Scratch paper or newspaper

1 hair clip

Bead cement

Assorted beads

1. Insert a piece of scratch paper or newspaper into the clip.

2. Place a drop of bead cement onto the top of the clip. Position a bead as desired. Continue until the surface of the clip is covered. Don't be shy with the glue, it will dry clear. Allow the glue to dry completely before removing the paper.

Blue Skies Barrette

Barrette backs are available in craft and bead stores. With a length of wire and some colorful beads you can create an elegant hair accessory in minutes.

12 inches 26-gauge wire thread

1 barrette back

Six 8mm glass beads

Six 3mm glass beads

Nippers

1. Insert ½ inch of thread into the hole in the end of the barrette. Bend short wire-end around and twist it around the long wire end to secure. Wrap wire around the barrette end once.

2. String on a large glass bead. Take wire under the barrette.

3. String two small beads and take wire back under the barrette, positioning wire just next to the large bead and positioning small beads on either side of the barrette.

4. Repeat step 2 twice, adding two large beads. Repeat step 3, adding two small beads. Continue wrapping and adding beads in this fashion until surface of barrette is covered and beads are used up.

5. Wrap thread around the end of the barrette three times, weaving thread in and out of the hole to secure. Tuck wire underneath the wraps and snip excess tail.

Beaded Hair Tie

Root through your drawers and find the salve in salvaging. You can dress up any hair band with wire and beads in just minutes. A thick hair elastic works best for this project, providing a sturdy base for the beads.

1 dozen or more assorted beads

1 dozen or more headpins

Round-nose pliers

Nippers

4 to 5 inches 22-gauge steel wire

Ponytail holder

1. String each bead onto its own headpin, or string several onto one headpin, and make a loop at the top using round-nose pliers.

2. Using nippers, cut a piece of the wire 4 to 5 inches long. Bend the wire in half. String on all of the headpin loops so that the beads fall to the center of the wire. Now cross the tail wires so that all of the headpins are caught between them. The beads should be clustered tightly together. Wrap the tail wires tightly in opposite directions around the metal joiner of the ponytail holder. Tuck the tails under the wraps and snip excess wire.

Feature Bead Ring

Some flat-sided beads are just begging to be shown off. This project will let you turn your favorite bead into a ring in minutes. Try making this ring using other beads, such as oblong freshwater pearls. Just make sure the hole is large enough to accommodate both wire ends.

Nippers

3 to 4 inches 22-gauge half-hard sterling wire

Ring mandrel or dowel

1 flat-sided bead

Hard-nose pliers

1. Using nippers, cut 3 to 4 inches of the wire. Bend wire around your finger to get the general idea of ring circumference. Wrap wire around the mandrel or dowel to form a perfect circle. Leave about $\frac{1}{2}$ inch extra wire on each side for wrapping.

2. Thread the bead on one end of the wire. Push the other end of the wire through the bead. You should now have wire exiting each side of the bead. Bend one end of the wire against the bead in one direction and bend the other end in the opposite direction. Wrap the ends around the shank three times. Use hard-nose pliers to tighten wraps if necessary. Snip excess wire ends.

suppliers

BALINESE AND TURKISH SILVER

Singaraja Imports

P.O. Box 4624

Vineyard Haven, MQ 02568

(800) 865-8856

Gorgeous contemporary and traditional designs in sterling. Write for catalog.

INDIAN SILVER

Taru

43122 Christy Street

Fremont, CA 94538

(510) 440-1496

Unique, beautiful traditional and contemporary designs in sterling.

THAI SILVER

Kamol

P.O. Box 95619

Seattle, WA 98145

(206) 764-7375

Unusual Hill Tribe and other Thai traditional and contemporary designs.

COPPER & NICKEL BEADS

Double Joy Beads

7119 East Sahuaro Drive

Scottsdale, AZ 85254

(480) 998-4495

Huge selection of copper beads.

Write for catalog

CHAIN

Kamal Trading Co.

2622 West Lincoln Avenue

Suite 101

Anaheim, CA 92801

(714) 828-0567

WIRE AND FINDINGS

Starr Gems

220 West Drachman

Tucson, AZ 85705

(800) 882-8750

SEED BEADS AND FINDINGS

Piney Hollow

427 Fourth Avenue

Tucson, AZ 85705

Eclectic collection of new and

collectible beads, mail order for

any finding you need.

GLASS

East of Oz

P.O. Box 665

Bronx, NY 10569-0665

(718) 798-7961

Beautiful German and Czech vin-

tage, antique, and collectible

beads.

GEMSTONES

Bead Palace

163 S. Madison Avenue

Greenwood, IN 46142

(888) BEADS-11

Highest quality of gemstones from

India, including sapphires, rubies,

amethysts, garnets, and more.

BUTTONS

Central Yarn Shop

53 Oak Street

Portland, ME 04101-3921

(207) 775-0852

OUTSIDE OF THE U.S.

The Sassy Bead Co.

2076 Yonge Street

Toronto, ON   M4T 1V7

Canada

(416) 968-0706

Pulp

348 Danforth Avenue

Toronto, ON   M4K 1N8

Canada

(416) 462-2812

Handworks Supplies

244 Chapel Street

Prahan VIC   3181

Australia

resources

MAGAZINES

Bead & Button

to subscribe, call (800) 533-6644

Beadwork

to subscribe, call (970) 669-7672

Jewelry Crafts

to subscribe, call (800) 528-1024

Lapidary Journal

to subscribe, call (800) 676-4336

Ornament

to subscribe, call (800) 888-8950

BOOKS

Beckwith, Carol. *Nomads of Niger.* Abradale
Press, 1993.

Borel, France. *The Splendor of Ethnic Jewelry.*
Harry N. Abrams, 1994.

Coles, Janet, and Robert Budwig. *Beads: An
Exploration of Bead Traditions Around the
World.* Simon & Schuster, 1997.

Dubin, Lois Sherr, and Robert K. Liu. *The History
of Beads.* Harry N. Abrams, 1987.

Fisher, Angela. *Africa Adorned.* Harry N. Abrams,
1984.

Liu, Robert. *Collectible Beads: A Universal
Aesthetic.* Ornament Inc., 1995.

My jewelry catalog updated monthly

www.guthrieminingco.com

COLLECTIBLE BEADS

Piney Hollow

www.piney-hollow.com

ANY FINDING YOU'LL EVER NEED

Eastern Findings Corp.

www.easternfindings.com

LOOK FOR BEAD SOCIETY

MEETINGS IN YOUR AREA

Bead Society of Greater Washington

www.craftwolf.com/bsgw01.htm

Northwest Bead Society

www.wolfenet.com

Bead Society of Greater New York

www.geocites.com/SoHo/Museum

USEFUL REFERENCE MATERIALS

The Bead Museum

www.thebeadmuseum.org

LOOK UP TRADE SHOW DATES IN YOUR AREA

Whole Bead Show

www.wholebead.com

GL&W shows

www.glwshows.com

Renaissance Shows

www.beadshow.com

Gem & Mineral Show

www.tucsonshowguide.com

THE BEST WAY TO BE CAREFUL WITH YOUR EYES

Ott Lite www.lumenlight.com

ANYTHING YOU'LL WANT TO FIND OUT ABOUT BEADING

www.thebeadsite.com

index